Parthenogenesis

Anthology of Poetry

Leonidas Kazantheos

First Edition: 2021
Rs. 200/-

Cyberwit.net
HIG 45 Kaushambi Kunj, Kalindipuram
Allahabad - 211011 (U.P.) India
http://www.cyberwit.net
Tel: +(91) 9415091004
E-mail: info@cyberwit.net

Printed at Thomson Press India Limited.

Contents

Part One

Past Time

The Plight of Odyseus

I woke on a listless lonesome sea
Held fast in a rudderless boat
There drifted forlorn endlessly,
Lain lulled in my barque afloat.

For the dusk was slowly falling
As the sun glowed red in the face,
And the sirens and nymphs were calling
From the depths of this treacherous place.

Without a wave on this wide sea
Adrift in a rolling commotion
No one I fear can salvage me,
Now lost in this miserable ocean.

For the flotsam and jetsam was drifting
From the wreck of the previous night;
Nor my gloom intent on lifting
From my mind or grievous plight.

Without a wind to fill my sail
Becalmed in a timeless ocean;
Without a breeze, a gust or gale
I lay faint in this cradling motion.

As light withdraws this eventide;
Within the sombre, foggy night
No loyal shipmates by my side,
No moon or star came into sight.

For the gulls were slowly circling
Searching for what I know not
In this graveyard bells were tolling
In the wastes that time forgot.

No land to starboard or portside
No compass for my earthly guide,
No oars to row against the tide,
No one to whom I might confide.

Then I began to think awhile
Of the lass who made me smile
When I was then so oft beguiled
With woman's charms and subtle guile.

So I prayed to the Captain of my fate
To save my useless prodigal life;
And when this trial has come to date
Return my soul to my beautiful wife.

Blind Love

Although 'tis said that Muses nine
Place words on poet's tongues,
And warbling minstrels echo thine;
To crown their mundane songs.
There lies no surrogate, no substitute
On Earth or Heaven above
In brass and drum or stringéd lute
For this transcendent and enduring love;
-The praise belongs to you!

Now, no one knows where it came from
Nor where it's bound to go,
It is a secret, silent stream
With its' own ebb and flow.
While others praise each others' love in vain
In darkness still they strove,
Lest so to vanquish all their fears and pain,
Yet for their temporal and decaying love;
-The blame belongs to you!

No earthly wonder could compare
With every word we breathe
Nor any magic spell impair
The secrets of your smile.
So if they say our love is blinded there
In my mind's eye it lives a while
In visions of your wondrous weave
-The light belongs to you!

Disenchantment

How can you say you love me
When you know me not,
Not in that very special way that is?
Your splendid beauty, though
It doth delight mine eye
Yet veils the flaws
Of your capricious heart.
And when that beauty fades,
Pray sweetheart what remains?
And what else might
I find to criticise in thee?
Were I to love in earnest and
Ignore those foolish faults;
Just as you my love no doubt
Exchange those flaws in me
For praise or admiration and
In awe of my largesse.

These gentle poets' words are
Merely garlands of the mind;
They're meant for fools, and
Are alas imperfect tools.
One look can say it all,
One single act, a gesture
Or some stance but will
Reveal the darkest truth at last.
It is the actions of thine eye,
Thy mouth and countenance
That educates my heart and mind,

The words selected and expressed
That fortify and edify my
Deeper understanding of your soul.
In these minute perceptions I'll reside and
Therefore say "No more of Love."

No more, no less lest I fall prey
To my mind's eye and then
Perceive in thee nor but
The errors of the world at large.
Yea love, I'll say no more of love, if
After all my love has erred;
Being servant to my lustful eye,
Devoid of your sincerity and trust.
That I have cried more as
A man than in the days I was a child
Should come as no surprise to you I know
For all that cry in love
May share my sorry plight.
So, my dear God strike out mine evil eye
And let me live in peace! Or
Should I reconcile my sore mind's eye
Unto the terrors of the beast within?

I might then know thee better
When I know myself being blinded so,
My lonesome beast now being wholly
Gratified might sleep awhile?
But, he'll no doubt awake and
Seek to satisfy his hungry soul.
A simple soul that sorely weeps
When you're not near to me.
Perhaps these words are then

Some sorry compensation for
The errors of existence,
The mortal errors born of fear?
This cankered grit that irritates
Mine eye might then in time
Become some heavenly pearl?
And that sole, shining pearl become
Some clear, undying tear?

Earthbound Love

T' is small pity that your earthbound love
Is but a phantom of the anxious mind
That doth delude the hungry, wearied soul.
Yet heaven's love is not defined by sand and stone
Or vagaries of wishful hopes, of longing or desire.
It hath but golden wings to soar beyond mere mortal frame,
It hath abundant voice to sing in glorious tone
And nimble feet to dance in tireless joy.

That I yet love and care for thee,
Despite your vagaries and common faults,
Is without question or mere doubt my love.
But I will have it known thou woulds't in time return
That love ten-fold to prove your love for me?
For I am met with brooding silence that conveys your doom
While you must struggle endless with your dismal room;
If then I must attend eternally in my own way
Then so be it, and so I might withal behold
The nightmare phantoms in your dreary mind.

While cupid's bow is drawn upon thy lips
Or soft, the lustre on thy frosty cheek doth glow
And stars divine doth shine within thine eye
So, I'll not plan to cherish your cold heart in vain.
In time I'll know the secrets of your sickened soul,
The miseries of thoughts that you hold dear.
I'll exorcise the demons in your mind,
I'll empty out all remnants of your pain and woe
And I'll have passions still'd, for the pure wisdom
Of the heart to grow and strength to show
Within my inmost, conscious being.

Fruit of the Loom

For the root of a ramifying tree
Is the source of delight in you and me,

And the trunk of a ramifying tree
Is the source of strength and majesty.

For the branch of a ramifying tree
Is the source of my tenacity.

Now the twigs of a ramifying tree
Are a form of stark embroidery.

Where the buds of a ramifying tree
Promise more to come as in our destiny.

For the leaves of a ramifying tree
Are the vibrant tufts of springtime's tapestry.

Then the blooms of a ramifying tree
Are the source of nature's ecstasy.

But the fruit of a ramifying tree
Is the cause of greed and all your misery.

So the seed of a ramifying tree
Is the source of awe and mystery.

Search Your Heart

I've learned to search my heart
To guide me through this present time,
I've learned to search my subtle mind
And to select the proper time and space
To play my poets' part;
I've learned to search my heart.

I've learned to search my soul
At times when I could find it
And hear its soothing phrase extol
Though you were keen to bind it.
I've felt the secrets in my soul,
I've learned to search my heart.

I've learned to search my body too,
Lest it might harbour any ill towards
My subtle heart and mind, they often do,
And if my conscience may remove
The conflicts borne of hate and love,
I've learned to search my heart.

I've learned to search my mind
Alas, too often I'd construe
With many doubts of lesser kind,
Our recollections now being blind
In fading memories we knew,
And learned to search our heart.

I've learned to search my heart
It's all a lonely man can do
To purge himself of hidden flaws.
So as this outer light withdraws
I'll feign at last a hidden, silent part,
And there I'll search my heart.

I've learned to search my heart,
Indeed my soul and spirit too
So now the final word is yours
When faced with all the options
Those closed or open doors,
The key to your solutions?
Is learn to search your heart.

If Love

If LOVE were simple then, for sure
We'd know the blessings it truly bestows:
We'd rid our life of sad refrains, begot of earthly woes;
Our wholesome love remaining ever pure.

When virtue lies in every thought and deed,
Or promise of a future time be met.
Then likewise your sweet kisses or your warm embrace
Would seal the bargain and, God speed,
There would be no cause for some sad regret.
For, as the seasons and the tides may turn,
Then our two souls would re-unite and face
The passions that in time do burn or lead astray
Like fortune's grace, so pied, go contraire on each day,
As winsome and capricious as you please.

If FAITH were ample in our mind and heart
As harvest baskets in the fall, so
Our dear souls then ne'er would part,
And happiness and joy would reign supreme.

Then our sweet lips would meet and trembling taste
Just once the pleasure on our wedding day,
Before those gathered so expectant round the kirk.
So bountiful, so full of worth, no more the days to waste
In restless hours spent seeking fleeting pleasure.
Then, surely bliss and joy would come our way?
Great store we'd place in our small treasure,
Not so beguiled by worldly stealth to idly lurk,
For, as they say with mirth in measure;
- "True marriages are made in heaven, not on Earth".

If HOPE were constant as the day, that
Shines most glorious as the Sun at noon,
Then our soft, spoken vows in time reflect
As does the gentle radiance of the Moon.

If

If we could only lie on the edge of that Boundless Ocean,
With the clouds of our unresolved fears
Passing mysteriously,
Beneath the smouldering sun.
Our twilight years absolved in the sighs of the crashing surf,
And our salty tears dissolve like sparkling crystals into the sands of
time.

And if we could but die in a frozen wasteland,
And then awake in another world.
Then moments like these would freeze
And our icicled eyes would plead
For the warmth of passion.
And our frost-bitten lips would then hiss
The word unspoken.

Love's Entreaty

Whilst to mine eye thou must entreat my virile fire unkind;
Nor to my constant but impoverished heart that feels,
Or to my reasoned and perplexéd mind,
You'll ravage space for your most passionate appeals.
And in composing overtures that no man can resist,
Forsooth! No doubt you'll find in me Achilles' heels.
So, my dear lady then I must insist;
I am your slave, and as a slave I must attend
Yeah, every whim and secret fantasy or tempting trend;
And to forgive your hidden flaws while youthful beauty doth persist.
For all is folly in your waning arms, I know
And love's delusions lurk mischievously in your sweet kiss.
For verily art thou a beauteous nymph I should forgo.
And I? Merely a lame man seeking some dear, solitary crutch.

Of all the crooked and divergent paths that lovers take,
One fuelling passion drives their engines fierce,
Despite the vows and compromise they make.
The arrows cruelly loosed and what frail hearts they pierce!
What lust is love, and what Love is not lust,
Though each mere semblance of a withering flame?
Lust is not love, for what lust will endure in purest love excluding
trust?
Although to most who seek to gratify their mind they're much the
same.
The latter love, in tune and harmony persists in Time;
The former, Fahrenheit desire spent all too soon.
Were I to choose or fate perchance command what's mine,
For who knows where an exiled love may rest in peace?

Or, should I relent and deal cruel fate a lesser hand;
And there, withholding all the aces pass this test?

Would'st thou wager all thy own at my request,
Or surrender a superior wit and any vital need for my dear sake?
Nay, that vain folly would condemn you to an endless loss;
From which there is no hope, no faith and so alas no love.
For love's sweet gift is fit not for some reckless triste, but some
secret trove,
So far removed from every idle, passing glance.
So in thee my love I seek not just to own or advertise myself above,
Or swagger boldly midst the populace outgrown.
What little that I am or own is but short measure when compared to
thee;
For your most bounteous and extensive charms I'd never own,
Hardly, had I but presumed to be some small discovery.
No greater treasure would I seek to call my own 'cept your respect.
For I in turn would barter mine, not least a meagre sacrifice,
To gain the love and wisdom of your most adoring soul.

Fire Of Love

So high entranced am I with thee
That naught else do I barely see
So being blind to this romance
My heart it soars and starts to dance.
- Is happiness returning?

So beloved of me art thou
That I still love you even now.
Despite the passage of long years,
The joys, the sorrows and the tears.
- My thoughts still stray with yearning.

Though I am common in a crowd,
With you I sense I'm standing proud
And in assurance grown quite strong,
Despite the distance of the throng.
-With you I'm always learning.

So enamoured of thee am I,
That I will love you till I die.
And in remembering every breath
That we will triumph over death.
-The wheel of life keeps turning.

So devoted to you am I,
While castles crumble and fortunes fly.
My love remains in constancy,
Now constant in eternity.
- The fire of love keeps burning.

All Good things Come to an end And then Return

Love's Lease

For me love's lease was but a span too short
Somehow it seemed to lack that extra yard.
Some length and breadth was all I sought,
Although so long I wished to love so hard
To swell voluptuous as this siren's song
To whom might this sad, vanquished song belong?

In my imaginary, lonesome song,
I've longed to love but loved too long,
So love imagined to endure has come to naught.
Oh yes, love's-lease seems less a life to live lifeless,
Now listless and so loveless to the bitter end
Oh Ares, stir my sinews strong!

The love I sought was not enough
In lacking constancy in sinew and in heart.
Yeah always seemed too rough and tough
'Cept when resigned to lust and turned to dust
To dust at last we shall return I'll trust,
Oh Great Hephaestus forge my will on Earth!

For me love's lace now lies enticingly alive,
Dark veil on flesh, my heart's desire
Her soft lips blessing nature's bud.
Some sacred token of impassioned fire;
Oh Aphrodite bless this band of gold!
And Eros loose your golden dart within my heart!

Ode to Lilith

Say that upon the sacred altar of her tender thighs,
You dare to place, a sacred kiss so sweet;
And yet it was impassioned with some sour disgrace.
Say that upon the bosom of her aching heart,
You'll sacrifice your pain, your tears, your sighs,
Assured at first that from her side you ne'er shall part.
These wholly foolish hopes will all the bitter seem,
When you last gaze upon her sullen face.

She'll turn and with one look, demolish every dream;
And yet in vain you deign to offer some solace
And stare once more into her transfixed face.
Your bones she'll petrify with dread and awesome fright.
An earnest plea or prayer perhaps might find some place;
You'll taste this fruit so sweet, yet deadly with delight.
How tantalising seems her languorous gaze,
Her eyes stare back into some far and distant space.

Say that upon her silken cheek or lips, rose-red,
You lay your solemn oath, your undying love
Yet borne no doubt of dread and unknown fear.
You may indeed solicit admiration or repair
The vagaries of love that wise feet ne'er should tread;
When hopes are dashed and you at last embrace despair,
You know your earnest, foolish vows
With love's remorse are held no longer dear.

Say, as you stroke her hand and frozen fingertips,
There is no other love that will endure

Nor e'er replace a love so deep.
When she has sadly gone, you'll weep so tragically.
You'll wonder why your flesh Hell grimly strips,
Now you're alone again in all your quiet misery.
Although, again you hope and not relent,
You offer more though now your heart it will not sleep.

She swears that she desires no other love so blind,
Why none so brave, nor generous there
In all the world no one she'd in her chamber keep.
While you caress and gently groom her tousled hair,
To soothe her restless heart and troubled mind,
She then invokes that evil daemon to declare,
"You <u>too</u> must suffer for my love in vain.
For <u>my</u> true love; all lost men wholly weep."

She then begins her ancient song alluringly,
"For I was sore dejected too my love,
By one so bold, before I e'er met you."
A song that did bewitch his heart and curious mind.
Tossed to and fro by wicked waves of agonising ecstasy,
And shuddering with an ague yet undefined;
He dares declare a sacred love so deep,
A love so strong and yet, so sadly true."

Secret Thoughts

Foremost in my secret thoughts
Lingers memories of thee;
Of the battles we have fought,
Wishing naught but verity.
Enemies without and those within,
Have lots to lose and much to gain.
Orchestrate their enmity,
Like the damp persistent rain.

Yea, what of Eros and of strife?
When, I have been the prophet of my life
Composing stanzas and similitudes,
At sunset sadly disposed of the residues.
At dawn awoke somewhat censorious,
With thoughts sublime and obscure moods
Worn down each day by some frail chorus
Of dour philosophic platitudes.

Awoken by some passion or desire?
The maid below re-kindles fire.
While I above, reflect on love
The lamp wound down, I sternly strove
In night-time's splendour to withdraw,
The latch to drop, now lock the door
On past and future periodic times
Bereft of reasons or of rhymes.

Simply put I cannot say,
As I'm apt to muddle through.

Was it me or was it you,
Was it pink or was it blue?
Neither, you might care to add,
But the ending sure was sad.
You the patient, me the medic,
As things turned from worse to bad.

Enlightened then by this prognosis
Of a mild itch and neurosis.
We came through the better part,
That which ended in psychosis.
If I ever loved again
Would it matter what endured?
Pleasure's fleeting wings bring pain,
Like that damp persistent rain.

Did you think this rhyme was wrought,
On some whim or idle thought?
Or the consequence of sole reflection
On this dire particular day?
Deftly, am I apt to play,
On its meaning or encryption.
Have it then as some sure sign,
The poet hath instruction.

Sappho's Song

Stay, for one more hour or one more day my love
Or better still stay here forever close to me;
Abjure the battle-axe, the spear and shield,
The roar of battle?

Oh, would that I might but honour bids me on
To join with comrades true in those distant lands,
There to protect the humanity that's ours,
The peace and freedom?

What peace might I possess in my night time vigils,
Or what freedom might my limbs enjoy back here,
Drawing pitchers from a well or milking goats
While you're waging war?

Would you have me stay here and plait laurel crowns
Or to pour perfumed libations to the gods,
While they suffer under the yoke of tyrants?
It's unbearable!

Well, my heart is heavy, but in truth resigned
To all life's burdens and to sweet love's bitter fruit,
That falls in storms, whose flesh decays what lies
In dark persuasion.

Firstly, it fills me with dread and secondly
With anger and remorse to think of all the
Lives lost in pursuit of honour in battle
-It's a tragedy!

Yes, it's a tragedy of intervention
The lack of harmony and education
The brutal agony with indignation;
Can we save the world?

No, it's a tragedy of their religion,
The lack of harmony and comprehension
A bloody parody, state intervention;
Pointless sacrifice!

Well, here is my Argosy and I must leave
You with your lady-friends again in misery.
I'll no doubt linger longer in your memory,
If your love suffice?

It's a crime to enjoy life while others die,
To enjoy life's pleasures on this distant isle,
While Assyrians shake spears at Athens gates,
It's selfish I know.

Now, one last embrace or kiss before I go
Fair Sappho, reluctantly I've made my vow
So, bid me well, and hopefully more loved when
I return to you.

Sleeping Beauty

Prince Gallant:
I used to think that slumberous look she wore,
Her flowing hair, the drowsy-lidded eyes
Were artless affectation, nothing more,
But now, and far too late, I realise
-How sound she sleeps behind her thorny wall
Of rooted selfishness and vanity.
Which, once I did dispel and deigned to kiss her lips.
To wake a heart so chill, as cold as stone,
A heart that ne'er would wake at all.

Princess:
I wish the Prince had left me where he found me,
Wrapped in my rosy trance, so charmed and deep.
I could have lain in sloth a hundred years asleep.
I shun this drab and noisy world around me,
The castle's thronged with lecherous suitors, all out-grown,
But none in this cruel world true-hearted, gentle, kind.
And worst of all, they've cut the brambles down,
Alas, the thorny briars I felt safe behind.

Prince Gallant:
I wish I'd left that fateful moment when;
Her gross enchantment became mine.
Soft twilight promised reveries of love's repose,
But now approaching dawn reveals my nightmare fears.
I see the pretty tactics and disguises that such vines employ,
To hide the poison barbs beneath the lustrous rose,
A form that doth endeavour to seduce, then strangle and destroy.

Princess:
He thinks that with a kiss and out-worn chivalry
He'll touch my heartfelt modesty.
Or maybe save me from the cloistered world I've known so long?
Those fairy tales are now his foolish dreams - he's wrong!
There is no magic spell this gallant knight can cast,
To break this bitter curse of isolation that surrounds me.

What spoils the fruit?

What spoils the fruit is veil'd inconsistency
A cunning worm that burrows deep inside.
What spoils the fruit is her inconstancy,
A loathsome canker that she'll carefully hide,
Lest Adam wish his fervent lips had never tried.
A cankered blight upon her wholesome charms and how
It grows anew with every season on the bough.

What spoils the fruit is talk of love but practice of cupidity,
Though many judge what pleasant form hath pleased his eye.
What spoils the fruit is her perennial duplicity,
Which turns his stomach with each yearning, unrequited sigh;
And makes him wish with every hour that he might gladly die.
What wretch can eat that poisoned fruit and yet survive
The sorry torment with which no man e'er can live?

What spoils the yield is lack of substance and sincerity,
A waxen fruit that fails to bloom or ease his hungry heart.
What spoiled the fruit was his rashness and impropriety
Though that he must avoid yet now from her he cannot bear to part
He howls aloud! His mind and soul are now a world apart.
The soft sweet flesh, the limbs so cool and long,
Is now a bitter tonic to his vanquished tongue.

What spoils the fruit is that dire proclivity
That lacks the nurture or the proper care within.
A hollow shell, a transient form devoid of authenticity,
A rotting, viral mould subservient to his mortal sin,
A moral tone of little worth with that slow, lecherous grin.

-   Say what robs the lover of their dignity and self-esteem?
    A vampire whore who cares not for their secret dream.

What spoils the fruit is sheer mendacity,
The lies and alibis that honest souls abhor.
What spoils the fruit? Gross infidelity,
A cause that's lost to those who promise to adore,
And say their love will always follow hidden law.
-   Now nature's law with all its tooth and claw
Rips through your tender drupe and hoary haw.

What spoils the fruit is their incapacity
To understand each others' needs and stoke desire.
What spoils their love is their stupidity,
In throwing passion on their mutual fire
His rearing steed her whining mare will then most surely shire.
-   For no good can derive as lack of love will mire,
Nor any evil from their hell's trough can retire.

What spoils the fruit is their foul hypocrisy,
Desiring all that lies between but giving none.
What spoils the fruit is their propensity
For sensual satisfaction which they gambled on,
And losing all the wholesome gifts they owned.
-   Now all that's left to say or do has left their mind
For all they share are bitterness and thoughts unkind.

What spoils the fruit is its corruptibility
That's rife in every fleshy fibre of its being
But that's the measure of our fallibility
In darkest matter we are apt to dance and sing
In this temporal kingdom we might then exist
The more to glorify thy spiritual fire.
And in exchanging want for need we never tire.

Part Two

Present Time

The Labyrinth of Dreams:

Our Moon is a melancholy mirror
Circling wild in a miasmic haze.
While man is a puzzling mystery
Trapped in a magical maze.
****

The Sun's a melodic inferno,
Lightening everyone's heart.
Our dreams a kind of limbo,
Which set man and wife apart.
****

Awaken, sweet child from your slumber.
See the golden wings of a Phoenix beating,
Its sweet breath rising in rhyme and number.
From King Neptune's deep oceans forgetting.
****

Now when all of our earthbound endeavours
Are worn down and been crumbled to dust,
Then will our true spiritual yearnings
Find peace in a simple trust.
****

****

Childhood Dreams:

Now here, The morning dew does not freeze.
But settles, lingering on the melting tarmac,
The scene awakens childhood memories.
As this big metal bird transports me back
Where once the rugged tracks of British tanks
Rolled through the urban garden of the Hesperides.
With vague recollections and of blanks,
I wonder what and who will greet me now?

But then I do remember times gone by,
When tribal conflict scarred Utopia's dream.
No matter now how hard I try
When reaching out to turn the garden tap,
A wasp had stung me on the tongue.

A scene that harkens my mind back,
Of winding lanes, and laughing streams.

Aurora:

Aurora, herald to the Dawn.
Was known to gambol in the day.
Even to her heart forlorn,
That Icarus's wings were wet with clay.
In vigilant, she slept-in through the knight.

And in the morning he awoke to find,
T'was only in his foolish dreams,
That she abashed inclined to stay.

Blake's Prosody:

In this state of transience
With the aid of transference
Are there any heaven scent
Metaphors at all?

But with gross alliteration
Or attempts at perfect diction
We can sort out fact from fiction
When we're up against the wall.

But when you hear my assonance
Then there's surely every chance
That your heart will long to dance
At the policeman's ball.

But if by all this happen-chance
You're not wearing underpants
Surely then by consonance
It couldn't rhyme at all.

I don't wish to cause offence
By grammatic elements
But the tense of this sentence
Makes no common sense at all!

In his songs of innocence
With his vast experience
William Blake spared no expense
In saying bugger-all!

In light of this experience
Of eloquent expedience
I see no impediments
To saying naught at all.

In a sense that innocence
Aptly rhymes with inner sense
Is there any bloody sense
In making sense at all?

And with increasing incidence
Or bizarre coincidence
Arose these tense impediments
Causing common sense to stall.

In defence of my offence
In asserting my intents
Note the date of this sentence
Has no future tense at all.

Sitting tensely on the fence
With abiding sentiments
Is by God a grand pretence
Causing Humpty Dump to fall.

With unlikely precedence
And alarming sentience
I sense that his "evidence"
Stands more than ten feet tall.

Is this simply an allusion
Wrought with conflict and confusion
Or some rhyming repetition
Wholly meaningless to all?

No, it has a certain cadence
Which evokes a certain
presence
That the poet has an essence
That's available to all!

Bonfire Night

Bonfire blaze
Misty Moon
Wilting rose
Pink balloon
Children's laughter
Parent's glee
Cold hereafter
"What's for tea?"

I've got pizza
And some wine
In the freezer...
Sounds sublime.
Or there's fish
At suppertime?
So just one wish
Before you climb

The wooden hill
To paradise
Where you might fill
Your hearts' delight
And languish still
In timeless awe
Both day and night.
The night before

November's plot
Seems awfully quiet

And were it not
We'd never try it
Nor disrupt the sky
With storm and fire
To please our eye?
This funeral pyre.

Pagan Pastorale

Honey is made by the bee;
Past bitterness borne of life's sorrow,
When we linger on tragedy,
We'll sure be sad the morrow.

At dawn in the bower she cries;
The Nightingale's song augurs sadly,
At twilight far she flies,
So I'll be gone more gladly.

The turtledoves cooing again;
In our hearts their melodies echo,
With every teasing refrain,
So tender, so loving, so mellow,

The meadow that blooms in the spring;
The High Field laying fallow,
A true purpose to everything,
A joy to every fellow.

Arrayed along in the lane;
Rose briers, the hawthorn and sallow,
Recalling all of our pain,
Still, just as well we're shallow.

Lust is God's gift to the goat;
Swift wings a boon to the swallow,
When I can find me a boat,
Then I'll be gone tomorrow.

Church Choirboys that murmur so holy;
The bulls in the meadow that bellow,
Sounding so dire melancholy,
They bring hope to every fellow.

When flowers bloom bright in the spring;
Life's bountiful harvest will follow,
Whenever church bells do ring,
We'll have faith in our tomorrow.
Swift fishes that swim up the stream;
Green frogs that lie in their shallow,
Are part of great nature's scheme,
With a joy in every - "Hello!".

Patience is quite like a shield;
To the gardener tending his marrow,
Or the farmer seeking to wield
The scythe, the plough and the harrow.

The weaver alone on his loom;
The blacksmith's raging bellows,
The pearly face of the Moon, and
The Sun, in brilliant yellows.

Lust is God's gift to the goat;
Swift wings a boon to the swallow,
When I can find me a boat,
Then I'll be gone tomorrow.
Along the murmuring stream;
The rowan, the hazel and black sloe,
Are all part of nature's scheme,
Drawing solace from every sorrow.

Love is a marvellous thing;
It finds a home in every hollow,
What you expect it will bring,
A firm faith that you can follow.

Within the rooftops and eaves;
Quiet haven to the sparrow,
Sail high the bright autumn leaves,
Awaiting my wheelbarrow.

The sludge in the sickening shade;
Where the wild boar is known to wallow,
The pledges that we once made,
Oft broken with the morrow.

The ravens, the crows and the lark;
A hedgehog that's snug in his hollow,
At cockcrow the dogs will bark,
Now I'll be gone tomorrow.

Lust is God's gift to the goat;
Swift wings a boon to the swallow,
When I can find me a boat,
Then I'll be home tomorrow.

Silent Poets

Imbued with subtle synergy,
Today a silent poet n'er can be
But if they dare to utter sound
They'll be condemned as Ezra Pound.
Though Ezra Pound is long since dead
And all the silent poets seldom read
We ought to cherish what they said.

A noisy poet, I mean "wannabe";
One who, baptised in mediocrity,
Breaks the still empty peace of mind
Of the unknown, silent poet kind.
They being happily deaf or maybe blind
To those pretensions left behind.

But the curse of stand-up psycho-babble
That spawned performance art
Gave rise to roaring ranters and
To scores of prattling railers that
On nights of open mikes, to false applause
Can grunt and groan and fart.

It seems we need this ventilation
To prevent our soul stagnation
To diffuse, distract sensation
To console, attract attention;
And presume our foul pretention
Meets the merits of an art.

Some People:

Some people are made out of paper,
Blown along by each daily breeze,
They skip along and caper,
With a cough, a splutter and sneeze.

Some people are made out of stone,
They never will budge an inch.
They know how to stand alone,
When others are seen to flinch.

Some people are made out of stardust,
Others mere idols of clay,
And there's those you just can't trust,
While others don't know what to say.

There's those who know when to act,
While others just sit and worry.
If they only knew fiction from fact,
There'd be no point in saying sorry.

Some people have visions of beauty,
There's some that have fears of false pride.
Then those who are blessed by God's bounty,
While some are just ugly inside.

Some folks are as fragile as glass,
While some are as heavy as lead,
There are others as bold as brass,
When others have gone to bed.

Some people embrace life's wonders,
While others behave like mice.
-Some people make terrible blunders
While some are as cool as ice.

Still more are as brave as the lion.
And those who are made out of straw.
Some folks are as brittle as iron,
While others are simply a bore!

A few are as gentle as rain-drops,
Still more as warm as the sun.
While some stand alone at bus-stops,
When others are out having fun.

-Some people are made out of snowflakes,
Their lives are as pure as snow.
But there's those who encounter heart aches,
And they have much further to go.

The Moment

I wanted to capture the moment when,
Though it always escaped my attention,
For the problem with the moment often
Is that it rarely gets a mention.

While grabbing my camera to take a snap,
The moment fades fast into confusion
And all that's left is an overlap
Of lightning strikes in life's illusion.

Somehow the elusive moment transpired,
In a moment it was gone who knows where?
It goes when you're relaxed or inspired
Like a lamprey, a pike or a hare.

As it flew through peripheral vision
Into some black hole of space I presume?
We felt a short moments' collision
An encounter in my empty room.

But, the instant I gazed at the moment
In a split second t'was no longer there
And I couldn't quite pick up its scent
But nevertheless, why should I care?

So I thought I was simply day-dreaming
For a moment I'd lost my composure,
It wasn't a moment un-seeming
If it simply lacked some exposure.

It's not shutter speeds that turn me to tears
Perhaps something failed with the aperture
So whenever the moment appears
Be sure in your mind it's a fixture.

The Thorn

I lament the loss of the thorn in my side
Though the twisted thorn in my tender side,
Lay cold and hard like an arctic tide
Left me relenting 'til I sighed
Left me lamenting still I cried!
"Please take this bloody barb from my hide!"

I regret the loss of this crown of thorns
Though the thorny crown of least renown
Was a joke for the crowd who cried aloud;
"We want Barabbas with his Devil's horns!
There's a suitable scapegoat I'll be bound
-Take this imposter to Golgotha's mound".

I lament the loss of his spear in my side
Though the centurion's spear in my feeble side,
Like a soothing balm to my wounded pride
Was in need of some swift medication
Was a boon to my dire predication
A balm to my bleeding suspension.

I regret the loss of my earthly estate
For my kingdom on earth was a big mistake
I was nailed it seems for my miserable dreams
On this cross of timber, but can't quite remember
What the judge required of these wooden beams,
Or what I was meant to dismember.

The Unexplained

We saw the tear, we saw the chasm of experience
In our time no one came to transubstantiate the grain
We thought we could even communicate
The pain of love that bound us all.
But we were dreaming, they were wide awake
In their nightmare daydream, still sleepwalking...
So we decided it was time to wake them up.

Oh, what a bad time we had of it;
Dealing with madmen, animals and innocence
Falling on our knees, praying for compassion
Seeking peace and understanding
Oh, what a bad time we had of it.

Falling into the vortex of ignorance and darkness
Dealing with insanity, beasts and children
Lying in our beds sexually conjoining
Falling on our feet, we made a quantum leap
Stronger than quantum mechanics could explain
We were seeking hope and glory
Oh, what a bad time we had of it.

But we endured, some of us even died
For it, but for those that remained
The challenge and the dream loomed large.
Far and wide, beyond all our anticipations,
In the end all colours fade away.

In the light all colours, all confusions fade
Like futile expectations ground to dust.
The love, still sleeping, bound us all as
We were entwined in the matrix of illusion.
We were no longer dreaming, we were wide awake
And the world was fast asleep, sleeping in its ocean
So we decided it was time to wake them up.

We grew horns and tails, we grew wings
And halos shining in the radiance of the sun
They were over-awed, and I think impressed
Yet thought they could restore the dream
Perhaps even improve our version of it.
In life or death we are invincible.

The Voice

I move my tongue and find my voice,
I stir my spirit and rejoice!
In prose or rhyme, in song sublime,
My mind recalls another time.
Another time, another place,
Perhaps indeed another case?
Of verse or line, so clandestine,
A sombre mood I would incline?
I lift the pen and find the page,
In remembrance of an age;
When pregnant pause or consonance,
Required a certain eloquence.
A foreign accent - that I'll wage,
Perhaps a gesture of frustrated rage,
With open vowels, soft consonants,
It has a certain elegance.

I move the pen, the pen moves me,
The lines appear quite magically.
Am I the author or the scribe
Of some sad spirit deep inside?
Enriched of sadness or the madness
Am I removed quite tragically.
I glance around, I am alone,
No other soul has quietly scryed.
Nor sensed the ethers or brought spasms
Where there was no solace found.
Another page, throw this away,
Another hope, another day,

In which to recollect, recall, forget
The thoughts that do confound,
That harbour menace in each syllable,
Entreating all to fade away.

I turn the page, my mind now cleared,
Relieved of inconsistency,
Aware that each step brings me closer still,
And each phrase surely finds itself,
Attuned to every tide and wave
Or every subtle frequency,
The muse has found me, and my
Small voice is still in me - myself.

She is not me and me not she,
But one voice in eternity,
Now glorious in a song well sung,
Our chorus echoes sweeter,
That singing thus awhile will bring
Us closer to our destiny;
And there to find another line,
Another verse to greet her.

Tongue Twister

A riddle-a diddle-a diddleo, a riddle-ariddle-epo
A video-rideo-diddleo, a kineoviddle-epo
A middle, a centre, a left and a right,
A riddle, a question, a puzzle-epo, a muscle-puzzle-epo.
A grapple, a shuffle, a tap and a toe,
The dibble, a nibble, a dibble-epo.
A wobble or topple, a topple-epo, a bobbly-wobbly-po
A nipple, a ripple, a tipple-epo
A tipple with pizza to go.
A ballet, a rally, a video show,
A riddle-a diddle, a diddle-eo, a fiddle a fiddle-epo.
A goggle, a toggle a toggle-epo,
A bustle, a tussle, a nuzzle-epo, a fussily-tussle-epo.
A stipple, a bristle, a bristley-epo,
A whistle when you say hello.
An apple, a Snapple, a snapple-epo,
A hug and a cuddle, when you have to go
A giggle, a wiggle, a peck on the cheek,
A hug and a cuddle, the moon in a puddle, a puddley-huddley-epo
A laugh at the end of the week.
A happily-crappily reason to know, a happily-crappily-po.
A nobbley, gobbelly, gobble-epo
A rubbelly, bubble-ebo, a bubbly-rubbly-epo
A snigger, a twitter, a twitteritoo, a sniggerri-twitteritoo,
A ranter, some banter, some sushi to go,
A single, a double, some bottles to go, a bottley-singley-po.
A cackle, some prattle, a cackle-epo,
A haggle, a gaggle and I have to go, a haggley-gaggley-po.
A babble, a dabble, a dapple-epo, a line a snort and a blow,
A bangle, a wrangle, a bangley-po, a wangley-gangley-po
A muddle, a puddle, a puddle-epo, a puddley-muddley-po

Weather Vane

So there, now know when
Either now or again
In the land of "Know-where"
Where the Known never knows
With some knowse or know-how
Just how the wind blows...
Or why some weather vane goes
So, so. So, so...

"So what", you might ask
For this wearisome task
Of poetry show with some dozy doh
Though you don't give a damn
For a magical charm intended for you
With an Allah-kazam and an Allah-kazoo;
Where violets are read
And roses grow blue?

Say what's that hippie shit
'Bout Buddha and karma?
Now you can't beat a bit
Of soul psychodrama
Now and then for a kick,
With some hippie chick
Who knows what to do
Or, whatever can you?
If you're not hip to the beat
Of this hippie trip,
Or can't stand the heat

Of its' rambling rhyme-
Then turn on and tune in,
Imagine I'm crooning
And drop by and see me
Whenever sometime.

Because I can explain
If it's causing you pain,
Or it's driving you mad
And you can't see the point
Of this poetry fad
'Cus it's making you sad
When it's going astray
With its' syllables all out of joint!
-What the fuck are you trying to say?

So then, now know where
Either here or elsewhere
In the land of the "Known"
Where the Known rarely shows
With some knowse or know-how
Just how the wind blows...somehow
Or why some weather vane goes
So, so. So, so...

Winter's Song

The boughs and twigs though bare enough
As earth has yet to feel the chilling snow,
Nor frost-lined ivies climbed so rough.

At evening time the rambling brambles show,
Their coarse leaf crawling on the ground
Where soft the cruel north wind doth blow.

But how the rain blasts swirl around!
Now pitted here and there in tiny drops.
A distant gurgling brook, the only sound,

Moulds the mounds of mire and stops
Its course across green overcoats
Whose foliage hides inside the distant copse.

Now soft, a simple song of trembling notes
Is all the winter birds dare try.
The bugle Moon at even-time now floats

So pearly white against the sombre sky;
So like a gem of purest hyaline
And pencilled blue so daintily.

In threads of silk that softly shine
Amidst dark silhouettes of boughs undressed
-I rarely saw her so divine!

Far on the watery, fire-streaked west
Yonder where the crimson orb doth set;
Limps sad in glowing coals and longs to rest.

I saw long streams and wisps of violet
And beryl-coloured ferns so dim;
I heard the moorhens quietly fret

Their brindled breast and yellow trim
With waxen coats now quickly run
Surrendering to the watery brim.

Out in the misty skies, the Sun
Sets fast, and my long day at last is done.

World of Wonders

I saw a lame man walking,
He was full of bitter gall.
I heard a dumb man talking
Of his rise, misstep and fall.
I felt a mad man stalking
And I wondered if at all;
If he'd finally got the message
If he'd really heard the call?

I saw a blind dissenter
In a room as dark as pitch;
Where no sound was apt to enter
'Cept the cries of a nightmare witch.
So she followed where he sent her
Like some old seasoned bitch
To a place that was wracked asunder.
Laying low in the self-same bed,
Laid out in their corpse-like blunder.

I saw a blind girl weeping,
Her heart was full of sorrow,
For the lad that was not for keeping
And the day that was not the morrow.
I heard an old man calling
On a mountain faraway,
For a flock that could not follow
And a wolf that could not pray.

I heard a lone man sighing
His heart was as cold as ice.
A distant bell was tolling,
I heard it tolling thrice.
And I smelt the bonfires burning,
In the fields of harvest mice.
So I walked in an endless rambling
With naught but the gambler's dice.

I knew that a flute was playing
A tune I had heard before,
In a field of lilies swaying,
When my mind was filled with awe.
In the knowledge of apotheosis,
In the wisdom of eternal law,
I'll return to my cool catharsis,
In the hope it's a sacred door.

Part Three

Future Time

A Quiet Drink?

In this "chicken shack" I'm losing my head
So give me a break from the cackle dread
Is anybody listening to what they said?
Gawd! Let's get out of this "cattle-shed".

They squawk all night saying nothing at all
Everybody thinks they're ten feet tall,
Despite the rattle, - it's prattle that's all!
They should be running some market stall

- "Aren't we important let's make them think"
- "Anyone here want another drink?"
They're rehearsing the next phrase while you blink
They're making a mess and causing a stink.

Oh, for a minute of piece and quiet,
Why are they yapping, I just don't buy it.
Why are they gabbing 'stead of being quiet?
"Shut up for a minute, why don't you try it!"

(chorus:)
- Well that's enough, where's my Kalashnikof?
They're spluttering, screeching then starting to cough
Someone's yahooing, he thinks he's a toff!
Better re-load my Kallashnikov.

- Well that's enough, where's my Kallashnikov?
They're giggling 'n sniggering, snouts in a trough
Ooooing and cooing, Christ I'm gonna get off,
Better reload my Kallashnikov!

Dealing with Your Demons
Dealing with your mother is like working undercover
I'm not your ideal lover, just trying to be your brother
Dealing with your demons is a full-time occupation
Dealing with your problems is far more than I can do
I can't give my reasons nor describe the situation
Nor forgive your bad behaviour and the stress you've put me
through.
Your fashions and your passions are merely an illusion
But I'm tired of all your fractions and your paranoid reactions
Your manoeuvres and your movements deserve further speculation
So I can understand your motives and your sly manipulations
I'm working undercover and then dealing with your mother

The Fate of State

These our minions of the state
Standing long in poor debate
In a game of give and take
Oft in time procrastinate
Caring naught for pity's sake
Tending to infuriate
In the cause of love and hate
Passing bills to recreate;
The same old problems yet again!

This my friend do not mistake
Human beings are merely freight
To the Greatest Apostate
Living large in his estate
Who transforms their love to hate
There his greed to satiate
And his ministers placate
So that they associate;
Their constant failure with success!

See the Lords there imitate
Nothing new and far too late
With their verbose masturbate
And their falsehood and their hate
Or their porn stars defoliate
Our common sense propitiate
Through the drawn-out media debate
So that we accumulate;
A permanent sense of apathy!

Not the masters of our fate
Just the slaves of Queen and state
Who are apt to obfuscate
And on greed attend and wait
So consumers take the bait
Thereby to perpetuate
From the cause originate
Nothing new and far too late;
One more illusion of the Truth!

See how they appropriate
Land and sea and sky my mate!
There's nothing left for us to take
Shackled to the working stake
Freedom we might merely fake
And their liberties inflate
Truth and falsehood to conflate
In this parody of state-
We're merely automatons!

So I'll not here deliberate
Any further on our fate
'Cus it's certainly too late
In this perennial debate
To change the weakness of the state
Or thereby elucidate;
What they say is their mistake
What they mean to orchestrate
Is chaos and disorder!

Frozen Sea

You gross assembly of unconscious beings
Why dost thou vanquish peace
From here and there?
Enslave thy errant minds,
For my small voice and muted ear
Are meagre competition for your
Prattling tongues and restless eyes.

Pray, prithee kiss thy elbow if thou cans't?
Or withold thy waggling tongues and
Enrich thine impoverished brows!
Give me but for one hour of your largest ear
And fix thine eye upon my countenance
So I might take my poet's axe and
Break the frozen sea within thy hearts!

Shall I talk about the weather
Shall I talk about the libor rate
Shall I rhyme about my brother
Should I alliterate of love and hate?
Should I talk of anything at all or
Should I keep my big mouth shut?
Will your ears be ever open
Would they really hear my call?

Shall I speak of inequality
Should I then condemn corruption
Should I just espouse morality,
Speak of justice and compulsion?

And if none of these should satisfy
Or perversely entertain you
Should I take my leave indignant
And bid all those assembled here adieu?

Nay, I'll speak my peace in earnest
As my conscience should dictate.
I'll neglect to mention weather,
Not least mention my poor brother
And for now ignore the libor rate.
The bow is drawn in full, the arrow loosed
So, I'll seize the moment you've enduced
Forthwith and to cite my revelations.

I have but this long minute or short hour
And my small voice and gentle tear
Are meagre competition for your
Prattling tongues and eyes that dance.
Give me but for one hour of your largest ear
And fix thine eye upon my countenance
So I might take my poet's axe and
Break the frozen sea within thy hearts!

Islamaphobia:

I'm gonna be bad, don't wanna be good.
Shudda, wudda, cudda? Ah would if I could,
Hang out with the boys, the boys from the hood.
Choose my prince charming, if only I could.
Have my own place away from it all.
Have lots of friends from my neighbourhood.
Parties and food - we'll all have a ball.
Yo listen all it's understood!
Now Islamaphobia it's really sad,
But Islama-good orriz-Lama bad?

Don't wanna be bad, I wanna be good
Shudda-wudda-cudda, Ah would if I could.
No longer hang out with the boys from the hood.
Look after my folks, like I know I should.
Ah'd drive a fast car with a muscular stud,
Or get married, have kids, would that ah could.
It's more like Ahm Miss Understood!
Now Islamaphobia, it ain't so sad,
But Islama-bad orriz Lama good?

Shadows of Lowry

Are they but figures of a light concealed
These shadows cast in flesh and bone?
Whose soul and purpose may yet be revealed
Within a frame of silhouettes unknown.
Strolling eclipsed within some frozen void
From what is stolen to some empty space,
They dare not raise their shiftless pace
Lest emptiness engulf what lies destroyed.
As shadows lengthen in their latter days,
Stretching beyond the sense of what they knew,
Embracing darkness in the light erased,
Just to imagine what might yet be true.
Now plodding slowly from point A to B
In their stylistic, dread monotony.

With nowt but direst thoughts in mind they strive
Their tax credits and benefits obliged to reap,
The weary drones emerge from this vast hive
In some rehearsed, somnambulistic sleep.
Now daily seeking some worth from the whole,
These feeble-figured, hapless misanthropes
Appear to seek within themselves some soul.
Yet, sadly nursing only weary hopes,
Resigned to Salford's centre and arcade
There shackled to the treadmill of slow drive,
Their shadows hover in the morning shade;
From nine o'clock, yes nine o'clock 'til five.
Alas, these match-stick men, monsieur Lowry
Are praised today for their simplicity.

But to relieve their hungry hearts they'll drink
With yet another faltering eye or ear;
Care not what other folk are apt to think,
Still deafened, blind and far too lost in fear.
Like ants that daily scurry to and fro
Their sanitised dark sides still plodding on
With nothing less than they can barely know
Of that heavenly phrase "Thy will be done";
On Earth, the lost and lonely withering gaze
Being so bewildered by dour consequence,
Exhorts the slang and catatonic phrase;
"We're sorted mate, throw out the fents!".
They're done, so now they punch the clock
And off again to clog along the dock.

With all the beauty and the grace mislaid
Their mortgages and loans alone to keep,
With all their promises and cash-backs made
They're little more indeed than pastured sheep.
Eye sockets fixed upon the grimy ground
While tethered in their factory-fed parade,
They ruminate and covet every pound,
When all else in the world they own will fade.
Content to grab the offers that they've found
And rarely o'er the chasm they might leap.
It's far too radical a step I've found
And for an anxious flock it's far too steep.
Clutching desperate on their mobile phones
What vistas reign beyond their comfort zones?

Laughter:

The gaggle, the screech, the chuckle too,
The snorting guffaw, the giggling glue,
The devilish cackle, the roaring blast,
The uncontrollable spasm, the jerking gasp.
With side-splitting groans or insane screams
On your funny bones and nervous streams
Of contagious laughter and insane jokes,
That sly wry smile from the comedy blokes
A chain reaction of rib-tickling pokes
The crowds' condescending meagre moans
In spasmodic succession both first and last.

Oh Hidden God:

That I am subject to intemperate change
And victim to fate's whimsy or fate's spite
Seems strangely undeserved of late.
Sometimes, when all is well, I wish the sun
Would ne'er set swiftly on that day;
And night, dark night forget to call.

For I am dragged relentlessly each year
Through winter's death, and then to be restored
In spring's resurgent breath and there,
Being softly lulled in summer's apogee,
Fall prey again to autumn's sick decay.

Oh that I, a magus on some stage perhaps,
Could freeze the beauty of a summers' morn
Or hold chill winds from tender flesh at bay?
Or that I might recreate from distant memory
Each and every perfect day, thereby;
Erasing all decay and misery in mind.

Oh, that I could with one enchanting spell
Command time as I may, to stop or start
As I dictate according to my will;
To pause, take stock of life's ingratitudes
Indeed, to change ill fate to nature's good.

There was a time, when time was young
When freedom was my only song;
Say God, I must have done it all!

I travelled far and I travelled wide,
I crossed the river to the other side-
Where the voice of silence still remains.

So I'll say no more of sorrow
Or her sister sweet despair!
In this empty, vacuumed place
The soul's voice, of necessity,
Recites its solemn litanies
Of anxious do's and don'ts.

An eulogy of griefs and doubts no doubt?
Within this dark and formless space,
I am and then conversely I am not;
Alive in someone else perchance,
Alone, where my dull heart beats out,
Beats out in perpetuity, but not in me.

Thus ends his days our bold Prometheus
Chained to his rock while vultures nightly prey.
Who, born to his trials by light of day,
Dies daily of his needless fears by night.
And softly in his beating heart recites...

Oh hidden God where art thou hid?
In stone or flesh, in every singing bird and living tree
Within the stitch, within the hidden seam
Within the fabric or the thread of nature's tapestry?
So, as your boundless mercy doubtless is revered,
Reveal yourself and end this timeless doubt.

Oh Hidden One why art thou hid,
In distant memory, in faith or mindless hope?

Beyond the walls of ignorance and mystery,
Beyond the walls of greed and degradation.
Entombed within the confines of my exiled self
Thy will incarcerate, thy silent voice will out!

All-Loving God how art thou loved indeed;
In every limb, in every leaf, in every bird and stone,
In every church and mosque and synagogue.
All-Knowing God who art unknown to all
How might we know with certainty
Why thou hast abandoned all to grief?

Oh Timeless Lord in boundless space,
When will we reach the further shore,
Whose compass might we trust on Earth,
And in eternity how ought we cease to be?
Will you remember what we did so mindlessly
And will the record of our days remain?

On Days

On days when I am in a daze,
In silent mood I sit and think
And gaze upon the paper and the ink,
Or stare beguiled and wonder if
I filed the nib enough and is it stiff,
Or should I pour another drink?

I gather rose-buds while I may
On days when I am in a daze,
And wonder when I'll reach a phase
Of cool uncertainty, in such a way
As I won't be concerned, and happily
Rest upon the lessons learned?

In night time splendour I withdraw,
I turn the key and lock the door,
On days when I am in a daze.
In sublime moods and inspirations I retire,
Examining the virtue of each metered rhyme
And quietly being so amused, I gaze....

But what's the worth of poetry,
The perfection and the patterning of words
In some sequential symmetry?
On days when I am in a daze
I gather rose-buds while I may
And smell them in a silent way.

For who can say with cool conviction

What a poet or a poems' worth?
And if the metre or encryption
Is more than just a million miles away?
On days when I am in a daze
My muse portrays a sullen gaze...

So I am ill-disposed to while or stray
Or softly still your aching ears
With all this mellow, mystic poesy
And drown you with my poet's tears,
Or share my lover's pains in sad essay;
On days when I am in a daze,
I'm in some kind of rhapsody....

The Caryatids

Women are subject to petrification,
Hearts hewn from stone.
In old age much older, colder.
Ladies! We need verification,
If you don't want to end up alone.

When young - so blithe and bonnie,
Hankering for her handsome jonnie.
Now resentful and frustrated,
From each bitter disappointment,
- Learning *nowt* but man berated.

Now, more cynical as the years progress,
So long divorced from her white wedding dress.
Still she expects the best, though gave her worst.
Nor to believe or trust in any man -
A breed corruptible, an animal that's cursed.

Walking the dog in the rain,
Holding in all that pain.
—"I'll never go through that again.
- This is definitely the last time!"
Yes, we've all heard that addled, sad, old refrain.

Rhapology

I'm not a goon in a balloon, ah'm far too slick
I'm not your toy-boy, just for one week
My song is strong and starting to wreak
I'm not your everyday gibbering fool
I'm just a dude, in a mood, feeling cool...
I'm not about to go back to school
Why that's far too bleak, 'cus you know Ah'm a Greek!
I no longer do that crack in a creek!
- I'm just a Greek, who's wrapped in mystique!

Yeah, I'm a bubble n' squeak, just check the physique,
No Charles Atlas clown, just Greek and petite
No breaking down on the road or the street?
Not last year's model nor broken old stick
I'm hot to trot, like a Greek classic
Jus' listen now to the way I speak
In extra time or by next week
I'll talk the jive and I'll walk the peak
I'm a Chevrolet - the new "classique"!

I'm not a whiz nor a geek, O'm just-a-freak
I'm not a cunt, I'm not a prick
I'm not a pony, with just one trick
I'm not a phizz, indiscreet, just-a-Greek
Withnail I izz, with mystique
Heck! I'm not a bore, I know the score
This is my rhythm, it's my technique,
My Eldorado that's what they seek
-Aah says, I'm trés fantastique!

Say, I know when to suck and when to lick
I know how to push and how to kick
Hey dolorrosso I'm not a bozo, Aa'm just unique
Say, I'm just like you, trés magnifique
I'm so surreal, it's 'cus Aa'm Greek
This is my vision, in rap transmission
Believe me this is no sad poet's clique!
If you've got the message - that's so oblique!

This is my passion, this is my song
Brother believe me, it won't take long
"He's so conceited!" - that's what you think?
Well this is my rap, and this is my drink
And I'll have another if you can pay?
So don't waste my time, that's what ah say!
Say, it's got the metre and it's got the rhyme
Now you've discovered just what I do
So, this is my rap - it's just for you.

Imprisonment

Now, I have studied well how I can best compare
These prison walls, wherein I now reside, to name
The daily flow of hum-drum thoughts laid bare
Unto the lesser world beyond my fragile frame.

For though that world be populous, yet now
My mind seems all alone and sorely separate.
Now I'll imagine these dual worlds doth show
As but two figments seeming less intemperate.

Through all those false perplexities by which we live
And foster all that weighs the heart and moral worth,
In my mind's eye, with my soul's breath to give;
I'll take one lingering glance at my life's dearth.

While some deserve and others might indeed presume
Yet none do foster me, who soldiers here disconsolate
Awaiting declaration and the axe again to loom
For my fate's final toll and her most solemn oath to state:

Prepare yourself and then make ready for your darkest doom
To separate gross falsehood from that which has congealed
In time and what has grown askance in dread and gloom;
Within your liberties there hangs a common fate revealed.

For no man is above another, nor is free to exercise
His power and his influence without recourse to abiding law,
Or is a sovereign to himself, whose domain is a bed of lies
Whose legacy derives from blood in tooth and claw.

All that rancour and regret is but a shroud and this calumny
An all-devouring shame when all is done and said by me.
Therefore I will endure until the last breath doth expire
And sleep takes me forever from this world of mire.